The Dwelling Places of God

A Scriptural Survey of the Places God Has Chosen to Live

C. F. SMITH

WESTBOW PRESS®
A DIVISION OF THOMAS NELSON & ZONDERVAN

Cover art work and design by Randolph Davis Smith, Jr., Savannah, Georgia.
Cover photo used by permission of Beth Bock, Savannah, Georgia.

WestBow Press books may be ordered through booksellers or by contacting:

WestBow Press
A Division of Thomas Nelson & Zondervan
1663 Liberty Drive
Bloomington, IN 47403
www.westbowpress.com
1 (866) 928-1240

ISBN: 978-1-9736-3111-8 (sc)
ISBN: 978-1-9736-3110-1 (hc)
ISBN: 978-1-9736-3112-5 (e)

Library of Congress Control Number: 2018907004

Print information available on the last page.

WestBow Press rev. date: 06/26/2018

Contents

Acknowledgements

There are some people who have helped me get this first book ready for publication, to whom I wish to express my gratitude. Working with the representatives of WestBow Press has been a pleasure. I appreciate the careful pacing, guidance, and direction all of them have given me on this my first journey into writing. My wife Becky has been a great encourager throughout this journey, always believing in me. She has been so patient and understanding through the entire process.

Also I received valuable feedback and editorial assistance from members of my Life Group: Jane Cox and Lillian Neal, and my wife. My good friend Dennis Meeks wrote some kind comments to be included in recognition of the author's ability and diligence. Finally, I am very proud of my grandson Davis (Randolph Davis Smith, Jr.) for the beautiful background and art work he created in designing the book cover. Davis is a rising high school senior at the Savannah Arts Academy here in Savannah Georgia.

Dedication

I am dedicating this work to the wonderful members of
The Adult Bible Fellowship Class at
Compassion Christian Church,
Savannah Georgia.
These faithful men and women have loyally attended this class for years, giving me the opportunity to share God's Word with them Sunday after Sunday. My brother in Christ and co-teacher of the class, Dennis Meeks, and I have been wonderfully blessed by their spiritual hunger and thirst, and their strong support and encouragement.
Thank you, ABFC!

Dennis Meeks is also a member at Compassion Christian Church, where he serves as an Elder. He has oversight for Adult Spiritual Growth, including all men's and women's ministries, as well as small group ministries (Life Groups), with several hundred groups participating. Dennis' life career was in the financial services industry — banking, insurance, and investments. Also married for almost 48 years, Dennis is co-teacher of the Adult Bible Fellowship Class at the church.

> "***Charles Smith*** has been a friend of mine for close to twenty years. I first met Charles when I joined the bible class that he was teaching at Savannah Christian Church in 2000 (now Compassion Christian Church). From the beginning, sitting under Charles' teaching, I was impressed by his knowledge of God's Word and his dedication to his preparation for each lesson. That friendship has grown over the years as I have continued to learn and be challenged by his teaching. Charles and I have also enjoyed fellowship outside the church setting. He has become one of my closest friends as we both continue on our spiritual journey, and now co-teach that same class. I believe this book Charles has written will be a great blessing to anyone who reads it. It will be a great resource for future reference and I recommend it as a permanent addition to your library."

Preface: A personal reflection

I have loved God's Word (the Bible) for almost six decades now. Beginning to read the scriptures seriously and systematically when I was a mere child, ten years old, God placed in me a love and appreciation for the stories of the Bible, and all its rich truths. That love has kept me coming back through all the stages of my life. I have read and studied God's Word intentionally, diligently, my whole life, and love it more now than when I began almost sixty years ago.

God has graciously given me the privilege to teach His precious Word for the last five decades, in many different settings. Early on, upon graduation from a Christian college, with a baccalaureate degree in Bible and Christian ministry, I was blessed to teach the Bible as a pastor in small church settings for about twenty-five years; later in life, after returning to education for a master's degree, I was privileged to teach God's Word to adults in a local church setting as a lay member for many years, and to teach middle schoolers in a Christian school setting. It was there that I taught the whole Old Testament in survey/overview format, and The Life of Christ.

As I write this reflection I find myself once again shepherding a small flock of God's sheep and reveling in the glory of God's Word on a daily basis. After all these years, there's nothing I love more than the story of God's interactions with man, and the glorious future that's ahead for all of us, as revealed in the Bible.

One of the ways that God has taught me to study the scriptures is to take a theme or idea, and trace its origin, appearances, and conclusion, from beginning to end, throughout the entire Bible. That is what I have done in this book. It has intrigued me to think about the places God has chosen to live, based on what we know about this from the pages of the Bible. I have traced this concept from Genesis to Revelation in this writing; I pray that you will find it as engaging as I have. I encourage you to read this book with your Bible open beside it, to verify each point from the scriptures, as you read. I pray that you will be blessed with new insight and a greater understanding of God's wonderful plan, to "dwell with us".

— C.F. Smith
Savannah Georgia

Introduction

The Bible Says...

From the very conception of the idea for this book, it has always been my desire to lean heavily on the Bible record, trusting the Holy Spirit to inspire me and to show me how to convey the special theme I would be presenting. While being imaginative and creative, I wanted to lean very heavily on what the Bible has to say, more than what I think. I have tried in this writing to present a reoccurring truth found in the scriptures from Genesis to Revelation. Many years ago, I remember being strongly influenced by the late Billy Graham's preaching ministry. He was well-known for a phrase he often used as he communicated the truth of what God had inspired in the scriptures. He would declare authoritatively, and emphatically … "The Bible says …!" I also remember how that years ago one of my Bible College professors in a class on the New Testament book of Hebrews, would often accentuate his teaching with a phrase that communicated his personal belief in the authority of God's Word as reliable, and trustworthy, and so very important. He would raise his voice and become intense in his expression, chopping his right hand into his opened left hand as if he were chopping wood, and say "the Word of God – the Word of God!" And now after all these years as a pastor and a teacher, my aim is not to tell you simply what I think, but to demonstrate its veracity and value by supporting it with ample evidence from "the Word of God." It is with robust intentionality that I present my case with "the Bible says …"

With that said, I want you to go with me on an imaginary journey …

A biblically-inspired journey; imaginary yet based on truth found in God's Word. It will foreshadow the events mentioned in Chapter 1 and elaborated on in the rest of the book. But here, I will forego "quoting" scripture, and simply cite scripture references where these things occur in the biblical record. (In the rest of the book, most of what I say is followed by scriptural quotations.) For now, I will speak from the perspective of a witness as if we were there seeing these events unfold, based on my knowledge and understanding of scripture. But please know that I certainly don't claim to know all that transpired in these events, or that I even fully understand all that happened. But this imaginary journey will serve to introduce you to the biblical examination that I have undertaken in the rest of the book.

Ready? Let's go …

1

An Imaginary Journey

The Garden of Eden … (Genesis chapters 1–3)

Can you try to imagine with me what it would have been like to be there in the Garden of Eden as a silent, invisible observer, when God came walking in the cool of the day and was disappointed to find the man and woman He had created hiding from Him? Can you hear the concern on God's part when He has to call to them and ask where they are? Are you able to detect Adam's trepidation when he reports to God that he was afraid because he was naked, and had hidden? Now recall with me that prior to this, God had formed Adam, the first man, from the dust of the ground and breathed life into him. Then He had created Eve by causing a deep sleep to fall on Adam, then taking a rib from Adam, made Eve from Adam's rib. God gave her to Adam and they became man and wife, as one person. The Bible reveals that they were naked, or without need of clothing, but that there was no sense of shame about it between them. The implication is that this was normal, for them to not be dressed, in their daily routine. But on this particular day, when God comes looking for them, to have fellowship and spend time with them, things are different. They are hiding from Him out of shame.

Why? What have they done? They must have done something dreadfully wrong that caused them to be seized with such a cowering sense of shamefulness. And that, they have. They have done the one very thing that God has forbidden them to do, and now have been seized by a dreadful fear of being in God's presence. As we try to imagine the fear and dread in Adam and Eve's heart as they hear God's voice calling to them, we must also try to sense the consternation in God's voice as well.

I will explore the implications of Adam and Eve's sin more fully in the next chapter; but for now, just try to imagine a time and a place when human beings lived in a perfect environment with everything they needed, and God Himself was prone to walk among them, expecting to have sweet fellowship. What we find in the early chapters of Genesis seems to indicate that an ongoing relationship existed between God and *mankind, in which God was actually present in His creation and with His human family.

*(I want to insert a note here about the use of the term *mankind*, as opposed to *humankind*, in my writing. I am not using the term *mankind* as an opportunity to express gender bias. My use of the word is intentional for at least two reasons. One, I am using it to refer to all human beings, both male and female, collectively, as the human race; two, and more importantly, I am

opting to use the *biblical* language of the NIV Bible translation, where *mankind* occurs 61 times, and the term *humankind* does not appear. I am choosing to be biblical in my expression, rather than politically or culturally inclined.)

The Tabernacle in the Wilderness ...

Now fast-forward your imagination hundreds of years later in Biblical history to the time of Moses and the Exodus. Very little is said about God's presence on earth after the time of Adam and Eve in the Garden of Eden, and through their generations. As one observes the stories of Noah and The Flood, the birth and rise of nations, and the Tower of Babel, God's presence is only observable in a few individual lives, certainly not in any identifiable dwelling place. Going on through the saga of the patriarchs (Abraham, Isaac, and Jacob), and the account of Joseph and the sojourn of the Israelites in Egypt, we find the same thing to be true again. God works in the lives of some individuals, but there is no stated dwelling place for God on the earth. And even when Moses is born, and the descendants of Abraham begin to cry out to God for deliverance, He answers, and once again makes His presence known in demonstrable ways, but still waits for the time when He will reveal His plan for a tabernacle, a dwelling place, to Moses.

Far into that story of how He answers, you and I find ourselves sitting on the side of Mount Sinai in the Wilderness of the Sinai Peninsula, somewhere north of Egypt and south of Canaan. Moses is with God on the mountain and we can hear God speaking to him. In Exodus 24 we learn that Moses has gone up on the mountain and it is now covered by a cloud. The glory of the LORD comes down on the mountain (24:16) and resides there for six days like a raging fire. Moses has climbed the mountain and will be there for forty days and nights. While there, according to Exodus 25:8–9 God instructed him to build Him a place to dwell on earth, a sanctuary. This dwelling place would be in the form of a transportable tent-like structure and must be constructed in the design and with the materials specifically given by God Himself! Let's listen in to God's voice on the mountain as He speaks to Moses: (I wonder… *how loud, and deep, and resonating, and engaging … that powerful voice must have been!* Moses must have been totally awe-struck as God literally spoke out to him.)

"The Lord said to Moses, … have them make a sanctuary for me, and I will dwell among them. Make this tabernacle and all its furnishings exactly like the pattern I will show you." (Exodus 25:1, 8–9)

A writer in the New Testament, the author of The Letter to the Hebrews, describes Moses as being terrified at the sights and sounds of God in His glory on the mountain, waiting to speak to Moses:

"The sight was so terrifying that Moses said, "I am trembling with fear." (Hebrews 12:21)

Now we leave the mountain where God spoke and move forward in time, to the day when Moses has faithfully obeyed God and has seen that the Tabernacle materials have been gathered, the furnishings have all been made, and everything is ready to be set in place according to God's specific design. We take our place out of sight nearby and watch the events of Exodus 40 unfold. God speaks to Moses and tells him what to do, and Moses, with his brother Aaron, the High Priest of Israel, and his sons, follow His directions carefully. In verses 33–38, we are told what happens as a result:

"Then the cloud covered the tent of meeting, and the glory of the Lord filled the tabernacle." (Exodus 40:34)

"The cloud" mentioned there is probably the same cloud that had contained the presence of God as He went with them out of Egypt (Exodus 14:20), and where God's glory appeared to the people of Israel in the desert between Elim and Sinai (Exodus 16:1); it was that glory cloud that had settled on Mt. Sinai and hovered there for six days as God spoke to Moses about His plans for Israel.

We watch and listen now as God's glory and His presence come to earth again and temporarily reside in the tabernacle, or "tent of meeting," as it is called in Leviticus 1:1. It is the place where God chose to dwell in residence for a number of years, inside this structure, in the inner compartment known as The Holy of Holies, or the Most Holy Place. Seven times (the number of perfection, by the way!) we are told that God sits "enthroned between the cherubim" that were constructed as part of the pure gold seat / covering of the ark of the Lord in the Most Holy Place. (This is mentioned in all these places: 1 Samuel 4:4; 2 Samuel 6:2; 2 Kings 19:15; 1 Chronicles 13:6; Psalm 80:1; Psalm 99:1; Isaiah 37:16)

> There, above the cover between the two cherubim that are over the ark of the covenant law, I will meet with you and give you all my commands for the Israelites. (Exodus 25:22)

The story of the Ark of God, housed in the Most Holy Place, inside the tabernacle, being the seat of God's presence in the earth for many years, is a fascinating story. Through the lifetimes of Moses and Aaron, all the way through Saul, David and Solomon and the other kings of Israel and Judah, the Ark, housed in the tabernacle, and later the temple, was "the" place on earth where God's presence could be located.

The Temple of Solomon ...

As we continue traveling through Biblical time and the story of God's dealings with His people, we find ourselves at the magnificent structure known as the temple of Solomon, also known as The First Temple. The preparations for the temple, and its construction are described in two places, 1 Kings 5–9 and 2 Chronicles 1–7. It was built around eight hundred years before Christ's birth, and stood for around four hundred years until its destruction in the 6th century BC by the Babylonians. This structure was much larger, much more ornate and costly, and stationary, in contrast to the (transportable) tent of meeting. The temple became the pride of all Israel.

Go with me to Jerusalem, to the Temple Mount, where Solomon has invited all the spiritual leadership of the nation to bring the Ark of God from Zion, the City of David, to Jerusalem, to be ceremoniously placed in the temple, in the innermost room, the holiest spot on earth (the story is found in 2 Chronicles 5). It is Festival time. Everyone, the priests, the Levites, the people of Jerusalem and surrounding areas, have come to witness this momentous event. The priests bring the Ark to its designated location in The Temple and place it there. Here is what the scriptures say:

"The priests then brought the ark of the Lord's covenant to its place in the inner sanctuary of the temple, the Most Holy Place, and put it beneath the wings of the cherubim." (2 Chronicles 5:7)

When they have done this (as we stand back in the shadows undetected), we see the priests coming out of the inner parts of The Temple. All the priests are duly consecrated as holy before the Lord, and the singers and musicians are decked out in their worship attire. One hundred and twenty trumpets accompany the voices singing the praises of God, focusing on His goodness and His ever-enduring love. It's a grand celebration.

As we are caught up in the praise and worship, something supernatural occurs. That glory-cloud we witnessed earlier descends and fills the temple and in it is the presence of God Himself. Here is how the scripture writer puts it:

"Then the temple of the Lord was filled with the cloud, and the priests could not perform their service because of the cloud, for the glory of the Lord filled the temple of God." (2 Chron. 5:13b–14)

As we continue to watch, totally in awe at the presence of God filling the temple, we hear King Solomon proclaiming these words:

> "The Lord has said that he would dwell in a dark cloud; I have built a magnificent temple for you, a place for you to dwell forever." (2 Chronicles 6:1)

As we revel in what we are seeing and hearing, the excitement continues. Now watching and hearing the great King Solomon, kneeling down on a platform almost eight feet square and about four and a half feet high, in front of a massive gathering of the people, he lifts his hands toward heaven and prays a long and passionate prayer to dedicate the temple to God (2 Chronicles 6:14–42). As we hear him invite God to come and fill his "resting place" (6:41), and brings his prayer to a close, once again we witness the supernatural presence of God. The biblical historian tells us:

> "When Solomon finished praying, fire came down from heaven and consumed the burnt offering and the sacrifices, and the glory of the Lord filled the temple. The priests could not enter the temple of the Lord because the glory of the Lord filled it. When all the Israelites saw the fire coming down and the glory of the Lord above the temple, they knelt on the pavement with their faces to the ground, and they worshiped and gave thanks to the Lord, saying,"
>
> "He is good; his love endures forever." (2 Chron.7:1–3)

Ezekiel the Priest/Prophet and the Glory of God ...

Our next stop on this imaginary journey is Babylon, where we find a priest named Ezekiel, who has been commissioned by God to be a prophet and deliver His messages to the rebellious people of Israel. (Ezekiel chapters 1–2). He is with the exiles that were taken to Babylon following the attack on Jerusalem in 597 B.C. The city has not yet been destroyed, nor has the temple, but both will be within the next decade. But before that happens, God gives Ezekiel visions of things to come. His story is told in Ezekiel chapters 1–11.

Ezekiel's Inaugural Vision

In my thirtieth year, in the fourth month on the fifth day, while I was among the exiles by the Kebar River, the heavens were opened, and I saw visions of God. (Ezekiel 1:1)

The visions he sees are of the glory of God, that is, His presence on earth. First, we go with him in the power of the Spirit, and witness God's presence in his sanctuary, the temple (Ezekiel 3:12). Along with Ezekiel, we hear a loud rumbling sound behind us along with the loud sound of angelic creature's wings and some strange wheels in motion (3:13, 1:15). As we follow Ezekiel in his visions, we witness … the movement of God's presence…

from within the temple,
to the door (threshold), (9:3; 10:1–5);
to a place above the angelic creatures'(cherubim's)
wings completely outside the temple (10:18);

> to the entrance of the temple at the East Gate; and finally, we watch as the glory of God is carried on the wings of these magnificent creatures (Ezekiel 11:22-23), outside the city eastward to a place above the mountain on the east of Jerusalem.

So, we leave this scene, witnessing God's presence above Israel, outside the city of Jerusalem, stopped above the Mount of Olives. Significantly, God has left His dwelling place, the temple, temporarily. But He will return centuries later, from the Mount of Olives, back to Jerusalem, and back to the temple.

Now we need to catapult forward in historic time several hundred years, to witness another divine, supernatural event. There we witness how God sends His angel to visit a humble young woman and man in Israel, who are engaged and soon to be married.

When God Wrapped Himself in Human Flesh ...

As we take our place in the shadows and watch this saga unfold, we witness a powerful angel from God named Gabriel come suddenly, unexpectedly, frighteningly, and appear to a young chaste, pure, untainted virgin. Her name is Mary and her betrothed (fiancée) is a man named Joseph. The angel tells her that she has come into God's favor, and that God is with her. And then he breaks the amazing news that she will become pregnant supernaturally, without the participation of a man, by the power of the Holy Spirit. We are in awe, as is Mary, as the angel continues to explain. She is to give her baby boy the name

"Jesus," (Luke 1:31) and he will be great and will be called God's son. One day he will *rule the world* from the throne of David! (Luke 1:32-33)

We also have the privilege of witnessing this same angel, Gabriel, visiting Mary's fiancée Joseph, to assure him that things are all above board and according to God's special plan. Just out of sight, but within earshot, we hear Gabriel announcing the plan to Joseph. He tells him that Mary will have a son supernaturally by the Holy Spirit, and to name him Jesus, because he will be the savior – the one who will save people from their sins! We also witness Gabriel explaining how this child's birth will fulfill ancient prophecies about God's presence coming to earth to dwell up-close and personally once again (Matthew 1:22–23.)

Just a few months later in our imaginary journey through Biblical time, we hear a baby crying. Now in Bethlehem, south of Jerusalem, we are witness to the humble birth of the baby Jesus who will be king one day. The surroundings are common, and the accommodations are barely enough, but we hear angels singing about peace and goodwill on the earth because of this baby. And about the glory of God. (Luke 2)

Gliding forward thirty years or so, we watch as a man named John introduces one known as Jesus of Nazareth to the public out in the Jordan River area in southern Israel. John declares to whoever will listen,

---

"Behold, the Lamb of God, who takes away
the sin of the world!" (John 1:29 KJV).

And then we watch Jesus ask John to baptize Him; as John is immersing Jesus into the water, and Jesus comes up out of the water, we see the sky open up and what appears to be a dove descending and lighting on Jesus and remaining. Suddenly we hear the very voice of God coming from heaven saying,

---

"This is my beloved Son, in whom I am
well pleased." (Matthew 3:17 KJV)

For the next three years we follow this Jesus around from town to town, watching as he performs one miracle after another while declaring the good news of the kingdom of God. He heals the sick, delivers people from demonic oppression and strongholds, and feeds great crowds with an amazingly small supply of food. Quoting Isaiah, the great and highly respected prophet of the 8th century BC, he declares to the people of his hometown synagogue that he is the promised Messiah, foretold by the ancient Hebrew prophets. From time to time there are other situations we witness that convince us that he is indeed the Son of God. He gathers a "band of brothers" and disciples them. It is interesting to watch as we witness the group's interactions with him, as well as individual members of the group like Peter, James, and John. From our invisible observation point, we get to watch the epic story of God, in the flesh, reconciling the world to Himself.

One week before Jesus' suffering and death, we get to participate in a celebration of his *true identity*, as we witness what has become known as Christ's triumphal entry into Jerusalem. A few days before he is arrested and put on trial, hundreds of his followers stage a public demonstration that begins on the

Mount of Olives and ends at his entrance to the temple! (Are you recalling Ezekiel's vision of where the glory of God stopped when it departed the temple and left Jerusalem?) They place their coats and pieces of clothing, along with palm branches along the way and create a path for him to travel. As he comes riding in on the back of a colt, the foal of a donkey, fulfilling the prophet Zechariah's words, the people praise and herald him as their king, saying "Hosanna to the son of David: Blessed is he that cometh in the name of the Lord; Hosanna in the highest" (Matthew 21:9). On that day we witness the very "glory of God" leave the Mount of Olives and return to the temple in Jerusalem. But once again God's glory and presence will depart, driven out by wicked men.

We watch as Christ's glorious life ends in death, at the cross, at the hands of angry religious men who have convinced the civil authorities, the imperial government of Rome, that he deserves to die. But just when we think it is all over and we are about to return to our normal lives, we get to witness the greatest miracle of all time, the resurrection of Jesus Christ! He is alive again! Just when we thought it was all over, it begins again! We follow the risen Christ as he reveals himself to those who had loved him, and followed him, and believed in him, renewing their faith and reviving their hopes for a great future. In doing so, one of the things we hear him talking about is the Holy Spirit. Jesus is preparing them for another visitor from heaven, who has been promised by his Father. He will empower them to be his witnesses.

We are there when he makes his final speech and then begins to ascend heavenward, taken into the clouds, disappearing from our sight. From a distance we see two men (presumably angels!)

speaking to them and we hear them telling the disciples that this very same Jesus that was now ascending upward toward heaven into the clouds, would one day come back in exactly the same way! (Acts 1:10–11) And with that, he (Jesus) is gone, and the followers of Christ are left to themselves. Thinking they might really be grief-stricken and gloomy and sad, we are pleasantly surprised to see them happy and jubilant, and headed back to Jerusalem to do what their master Jesus had told them to do.

The Promise of the Father is delivered …

In just a short time on our imaginary journey, about ten days later, we are standing in the shadows of a place called the Upper Room, in Jerusalem, where a group of followers of Christ are gathered and praying. We hear this sound of strong wind begin to blow through the area. It fills the Upper Room and then we see flames of fire above each person. We hear them begin to praise and glorify God in languages they have never learned, as they are empowered by the Holy Spirit. We discover by quiet observation and later by some of the apostles' teaching and preaching, that this is the beginning of the fulfillment of Jesus' and his Father's promise to send the Holy Spirit from heaven, to take up residence on earth! Jesus has gone, but the Spirit has come, just as Jesus had promised!

The Rest of the Story …

From here we move forward in time, at the speed of light, into the future. We find ourselves more than two thousand years removed from our angel visit in Nazareth, and a virgin-birth.

We leave behind us the life, death, resurrection, and ascension of Jesus, and our witnessing of the coming of the Holy Spirit back to earth.

Now we are back in *the present day*, but conscious that we are rapidly approaching the end of all things, moving into a time period known specifically only to God Himself. We can't go there, even in our imagination, except to peer through the lens of what has been prophetically written. We cannot possibly hear everything that is said and all that happens. On this part of the journey, we must rely on the word of the ancient Hebrew prophets of the Old Testament period, as well as the Jewish apostles of the New Testament era, to give us snippets and pieces of information about what is to come. In the rest of this book, I have endeavored to document biblically what we have attempted to imagine together. At some point in the future Christ will return to earth as King above all kings and will have supreme authority over the entire planet. A thousand years of peace and prosperity will see the knowledge of the Lord become prevalent and common. If I understand scripture correctly, another temple will be built in Jerusalem (Ezekiel 40–48), from which a living river will flow (Ezekiel 47), and Jerusalem will have a new name that reveals that God is dwelling there again (Ezekiel 48:35). At some point in time near the end of the one-thousand-year reign of Christ, Satan will attempt one last uprising against God's anointed one, King Jesus, and will be utterly, permanently, eternally, defeated (Revelation 20). At that time, the final judgment will occur, followed by the descent of a city known as New Jerusalem, coming down out of heaven from God.

> And I John saw the holy city, new Jerusalem, coming down from God out of heaven, prepared as a bride adorned for her husband. And I heard a great voice out of heaven saying, Behold, the tabernacle of God is with men, and he will dwell with them, and they shall be his people, and God himself shall be with them, and be their God. (Revelation 21:2–3 KJV)

The biblical story of God's dealings with mankind ends in Revelation 21–22, with the LORD God Almighty (i.e., God the Father) and the Lamb (i.e., Jesus Christ) taking the place of the temple in mankind's experience of eternity.

> And I saw no temple therein: for the Lord God Almighty and the Lamb are the temple of it. And there shall be no more curse: but the throne of God and of the Lamb shall be in it; and his servants shall serve him: And they shall see his face; (Revelation 21:22; 22:3–4 KJV)

This brings us full-circle from God's presence with Adam and Eve in Eden at creation, to God's dwelling with us again in the New Heavens and New Earth in the future, in eternity. I pray that you will be blessed as we travel through scripture now to consider all the places God has chosen to live, between Eden and New Jerusalem!

2

God's Address

Where does God live?

Has this thought ever crossed your mind?

Have you ever seriously pondered this idea of God's location or address?

If you are like me and many other Christians, you may always have accepted and assumed, without doubt or second thought, that God, the Almighty and the Father of our Lord Jesus Christ, lives in heaven. And with that knowledge, you are comfortable and content. And beyond that belief and assumption, you may have never given it another thought.

At some point as a young Bible-reading Christ follower, I came into the knowledge and understanding of God's *omnipresence.* I think I was a teenager when I was first exposed to the theology of God's omnipresence, omniscience, and omnipotence—i.e., that He is present everywhere at all times, has all knowledge and is all knowing at all times, and that He is all powerful, having all power at all times. In this He is unique; this can be said of no one but God. The psalmist speaks to the majesty of the Lord's omnipresence:

Where can I go from your Spirit?
Where can I flee from your presence?
If I go up to the heavens, you are there;
if I make my bed in the depths, you are there.
If I rise on the wings of the dawn,
if I settle on the far side of the sea,
even there your hand will guide me,
your right hand will hold me fast.
If I say, "Surely the darkness will hide me
and the light become night around me,"
even the darkness will not be dark to you;
the night will shine like the day,
for darkness is as light to you. (Psalm 139:7–12)

So, if He is indeed *omnipresent*, capable of being in all places at all times, does He indeed have one specific place that He calls home?

God's Main Address

Without disavowing this truth of His *omnipresence*, when I think of Him as a personal being and a living entity, I still think of Him in somewhat humanlike terms, as far as where He dwells or lives, or makes His base of operations. It just seems logical that

He must have a place somewhere that He calls home. And as I mentioned earlier, that place is heaven. Now I do not know where heaven is, exactly, but I must assume that it is somewhere outside the reach of our GPS here on the earth—it is either outside and beyond our known universe, or it is so very far away within the confines of our ever-expanding universe that we can neither see it nor travel to it under our current circumstances. But the scriptures do clearly state repeatedly that heaven is God's main address.

When God was giving Moses instruction for the people after he had led them out of Egypt, we read these words: "Then the Lord said to Moses, 'Tell the Israelites this: 'You have seen for yourselves that I have spoken to you *from heaven*:'" (Exodus 20:22- italics mine) Notice that God wanted them to know where the message was coming from—from Himself—in heaven! Following below are a few references that support the fact of God's presence in heaven:

- Psalm 93:2 declares that God's throne was established long ago and that He existed from all eternity.
- Psalm 103:19 acknowledges that God established His throne in heaven and that His kingdom rules over everything.
- Psalm 47:8 states that God is reigning over nations and is seated on His holy throne.
- Psalm 33:14 reveals that from where God lives He is able to see and to look down on the people of the earth!
- Psalm 11:4 reveals that King David believed that God was ruling on His throne in heaven and from there was observing and examining human beings.

- The prophet Isaiah cites God as claiming that heaven was His throne and earth was His footstool; "This is what the Lord says: Heaven is my throne, and the earth is my footstool." (Isaiah 66:1)
- Isaiah asks God to "look down from heaven, and behold from the habitation of thy holiness and of thy glory."(Isaiah 63:15 KJV)

These scriptures are just a sampling to identify where God has lived from eternity past into the present—that is, where He dwells, and the place from which He works. There are more references in the final book of the Bible, the book of Revelation, that identify God as being in heaven at the final consummation of all things. There we see God sitting, enthroned, speaking, and being worshipped (Revelation 1:4; 3:12; 4:1–10; 7:9–10).

In the Garden of Eden

As I think back to the creation narrative in Genesis, when God created the heavens and the earth and then also created human beings in His own image and likeness, it seems to me that God's intention at that point in time may have been to "dwell" or to live with human beings on the earth. According to the story in Genesis chapters 2 and 3, the Garden of Eden was a perfect habitat and God was there with his creation, including the people he had made:

> But when Adam and Eve sinned, they had to be separated from God's presence because of their fallen nature, and it changed everything. (Genesis 3:24–25)

God banished Adam and his wife from the garden and posted fierce warrior angels with flashing and flaming swords to guard the entrance to the Tree of Life (Genesis 3:24). Under the penalty of disobedience, the man and the woman were barred from the Tree of Life and placed under the curse of sin; woman would always suffer the effects of sin in childbearing, and man would be forced to work hard and bring produce from the land by the sweat of his brow his whole life, and then return to dust (Genesis 3:14–24). And there would always be enmity between the serpent's offspring and woman's offspring.

In the New Heavens and New Earth

It is extremely interesting to me that when we come to the very end of the biblical account of God dealing with mankind, to the book of Revelation, God creates a new heaven and a new earth, brings a holy city down to the earth out of heaven, and recreates practically the same setting that we see in the Garden of Eden to begin with. Though thousands of years apart, the similarities of that future creation to the first creation, when God placed human beings in a wonderful garden, causes one to think that what we see in Revelation may have been what God intended at the beginning, in the garden. There will be a river running through the city. The tree of life will be on either side of the river. Nothing that offends

God will be tolerated there. And best of all, God Himself will be there to "dwell" with His people (Revelation 21–22).

God's Dwelling Places

God has chosen in His sovereignty to visit mankind repeatedly and to make a way to "dwell" with us, in varying ways and at different time periods. As we work our way through scripture in this book, I want to show you the primary places God has chosen to dwell on the earth from one time period to another.

In the chapters ahead, we will survey scripture and examine the various ways in which God has formed a sanctuary (a *dwelling* place) for Himself. He has always had a temple to dwell in—from an elaborate tent in the wilderness, to an ornate gold-filled temple, to human flesh. But God has always provided Himself a place to dwell with humans on the earth. And He will continue to do so on into the eternal future. The examination and understanding of how He has done this will deepen your love for God Himself, and it will cause you to marvel at His glorious plan through time and eternity.

We will look at God's presence manifested to Israel in the tabernacle during the period of their wandering in the wilderness, following their exodus from Egypt, and also during their entrance into and occupation of Canaan, the land that God had promised them.

Then we will take note of the kingdom period when Israel was united under the kings, David and Solomon; during this time,

David had it in his heart to build God a more glorious dwelling place (viz., the temple).

God allowed Solomon to construct a temple as a place where He would dwell. Following Israel's time of falling away from God during the period of the divided kingdom, God allowed outside forces to destroy Solomon's temple and the nation of Israel.

After being carried away captive and exiled, and then allowed to return to Judah, the Israelites rebuilt the temple, which remained until the time of Christ. About forty years after Christ's death, in AD 70, less than five hundred years following its construction, *this temple* would also be destroyed by the Roman Empire.

But before this would happen, God sent His Son, Jesus, who became *His dwelling place* and a new and different kind of temple for God.

When Jesus died, rose again, and returned to heaven, He sent the Holy Spirit back to the earth to take up residence inside all believers who would become followers of Christ; according to the apostle Paul, they would become, and now are, "the temple of the living God." (2 Corinthians 6:16)

According to scripture, yet *another* temple is to be built that will become the focal point of God's presence on the earth. This temple is described by Ezekiel the prophet (Ezekiel 40–48), and it is referred to by other prophets and apostles.

But, with the descent of the holy city as described in Revelation 21, there will be "no temple," but God Himself will "dwell with people". "And I heard a loud voice from the throne saying, "Look!

God's dwelling place is now among the people, and he will dwell with them. They will be his people, and God himself will be with them and be their God." (Revelation 21:3)

Come and go with me as we journey to each of these holy places in the history of God manifesting His presence and "dwelling" with mankind.

3

The Temple in Heaven

I want us to think about the fact that the Bible reveals that there is a temple *in heaven.*

The book of Revelation refers to *this temple* several times. There, in the unfolding of the apocalypse, it has a central place and significant acknowledgement. It is also referred to in both the *Old Testament* and the *New Testament*, in *Psalms*, and in *Hebrews*. Later in this chapter we will consider these references to *that temple.*

The very fact that there *is* a *temple* in Heaven is an arresting concept for me.

I wonder…*Why would God even have a temple in Heaven?*

—when, according to Psalm 24:1 – "The earth is the Lord's, and the fulness thereof; the world, and they that dwell therein." And in Isaiah 66:1 the earth is His footstool, and according to

Psalm 103:19 God's kingdom rules and reigns and has authority over everything!

Thinking about passages of scripture that state how great God is above His creation, and His vastness and power, it just seems strange that God would need or want a *temple*. Why a temple? Why is there such an emphasis on the concept of *temple* throughout the scriptures? Apparently, the concept of temple, the place where God chooses to dwell, is the epicenter of God's universe. I don't mean literally, in the sense of geography, but spiritually, in the sense of a divine headquarters. Psalm 11:4 seems to imply this idea. "The Lord is in his holy temple; the Lord is on his heavenly throne. He observes everyone on earth; his eyes examine them."

This concept of a place, a dwelling place, where God can be present, and dwell with others, literally encompasses the whole of the sacred writ, from Genesis to Revelation. The concept begins in heaven, and later extends to locations on earth as well.

Based on the Psalm 11 passage, we can speculate that God is ruling the universe from His holy temple, *the one that is in heaven*. To reiterate, the psalm says,

> "The Lord is in his holy temple; the Lord is on his heavenly throne …" (Psalm 11:4)

Note here, the Psalmist says … "his heavenly throne". So, we know the writer is not referring to the earthly temple that was existent in Jerusalem in the days of his writing. And, the concept of a throne is that of judgment and power, authority, and rulership.

The Psalmist confirms that The Lord is the one on that throne:

> "The Lord has established his throne in heaven,
> and his kingdom rules over all.
>
> Praise the Lord, you his angels, you mighty ones who do his bidding, who obey his word. Praise the Lord, all his heavenly hosts, you his servants who do his will.
>
> Praise the Lord, all his works everywhere in his dominion. Praise the Lord, my soul." (Psalm 103:19–22)

This is the idea conveyed in the Book of Revelation when we survey the passages that depict The Almighty God;

> John says, "And immediately I was in the spirit: and, behold, a throne was set in heaven, and one sat on the throne." (Revelation 4:2)
>
> Following that verse for the next eight verses, we have the Apostle John's description of The Almighty.
>
> John continues, "Therefore are they before the throne of God, and serve him day and night ***in his temple*** (emphasis mine) and he that sitteth on the throne shall dwell among them." (4:2, 7:15 KJV)

In addition to the apostle John's experience of seeing The Lord in His temple, the prophet Isaiah also had a vision in which he saw The Lord sitting in this temple and the angels surrounding Him, declaring his glory and holiness:

> "In the year that king Uzziah died I saw also the Lord sitting upon a throne, high and lifted up, and his train filled ***the temple.*** (emphasis mine) Above it stood the seraphims: each one had six wings; with twain he covered his face, and with twain he covered his feet, and with twain he did fly. And one cried unto another, and said, Holy, holy, holy, is the Lord of hosts: the whole earth is full of his glory." (Isaiah 6:1–3 KJV)

Notice there in Isaiah 6:1 that this was a vision of the Lord in the heavenly temple. This vision corresponds and agrees with the statements cited in both Revelation 4 and Psalms 11 and 103.

In the rest of this chapter I want us to consider two things:

> first, the biblical description of the temple in heaven that we find in the book of Revelation;
>
> and second, the references in Hebrews to the tabernacle, that explain that the tabernacle and temple which were built on earth at God's instruction, were "copies" of the one in heaven.

First, we look at *the temple* in Revelation...

In the twenty-two chapters of Revelation there are twelve references to a temple, according to my search using Bible Gateway. Possibly one of these refers to a temple on earth that is to be rebuilt just before Christ returns. The others very specifically identify *a temple that exists in heaven*, and which is a center of divine activity. Here they are, followed by some observations about what is said. (***emphasis*** in each passage cited is mine)

- Rev. 7:15 Therefore, "they are <u>before the throne of God</u> and serve him day and night ***in his temple***; and <u>he who sits on the throne</u> will shelter them with his presence.
- Rev. 11:19 Then ***God's temple in heaven was opened***, and within his temple was seen the ark of his covenant. And there came flashes of lightning, rumblings, peals of thunder, an earthquake and a severe hailstorm.
- Rev. 14:15 ***Then another angel came out of the temple*** and called in a loud voice to him who was sitting on the cloud, "Take your sickle and reap, because the time to reap has come, for the harvest of the earth is ripe."
- Rev. 14:17 ***Another angel came out of the temple in heaven***, and he too had a sharp sickle
- Rev. 15:5 After this I looked, and ***I saw in heaven the temple***—that is, the tabernacle of the covenant law—and it was opened.

Here it is interesting to note the old King James translation of 15:5: "And after that I looked, and, behold, ***the temple of the***

tabernacle of the testimony in heaven was opened:" (emphasis mine).

Continuing the Revelation references to a heavenly temple …

- (15:8) "And the temple was filled with smoke from the glory of God, and from his power; and no man was able to enter into the temple, till the seven plagues of the seven angels were fulfilled."
- (16:1) "And I heard a great voice out of the temple saying to the seven angels, Go your ways, and pour out the vials of the wrath of God upon the earth."
- (16:17) "And the seventh angel poured out his vial into the air, and there came a great voice out of the temple of heaven, from the throne, saying, It is done."
  (15:8; 16:1; 16:17 KJV)

In surveying these passages, I have some ***observations***: (all the following references are in the book of Revelation.)

1. It is clear to me that there *is* a temple in heaven, and it is God's. (11:19, 7:15, 15:5)
2. It is a place of service, and of shelter. (7:15)
3. The Ark of God's Covenant is there, connecting it with what God had instructed to be built on earth for relating to His people. (11:19 and 15:5)
4. It is surrounded at times by violent natural phenomena. (11:19)
5. Angels were witnessed by John, the writer, coming out of that place. (14:15; 14:17)

6. Voices, sometimes loud voices, can be heard coming from the temple, giving the order for judgment on earth. (16:1, 16:17)
7. The place was filled with smoke from the glory of God and His power, and the temple was temporarily closed, allowing no entry for a short time. (15:8)
8. An announcement that the judgment was complete came from inside the temple. (16:17)

From the preceding observations, let's summarize in a more general way.

There is a *real place* in heaven where God's throne is and where he exercises absolute authority over all things. It has servants both human and supernatural. There is activity witnessed there by the Apostle John. It houses the ark of God's covenant. Angels come and go, doing God's bidding. Sometimes activity is accompanied by violent natural sights and sounds like flashes of lightning, rumblings, peals of thunder, an earthquake and a severe hailstorm. This place is referred to and identified as God's temple in heaven.

Now let's move on to references to this temple in the New Testament writings, *the book of Hebrews.*

There we discover that what God had instructed Moses to build on earth as a tabernacle in the wilderness, and later gave the same instruction to Israel for a temple during the time of Solomon, was actually a "copy" of the true temple in heaven!

The writer of Hebrews says,

> "Now the main point of what we are saying is this:
>
> We do have such a high priest, who sat down at the right hand of the throne of the Majesty in heaven, and who serves in *the sanctuary, the true tabernacle set up by the Lord*, not by a mere human being. Every high priest is appointed to offer both gifts and sacrifices, and so it was necessary for this one also to have something to offer. If he were on earth, he would not be a priest, for there are already priests who offer the gifts prescribed by the law. *They serve at a sanctuary that is a copy and shadow of what is in heaven*. (emphasis mine). This is why Moses was warned when he was about to build the tabernacle: "See to it that you make everything according to the pattern shown you on the mountain."" (Hebrews 8:1–5)

In the ninth chapter of Hebrews, the writer repeats the fact that the earthly tabernacle arrangement was only a copy of the true one in heaven:

> "It was necessary, then, for the copies of the heavenly things to be purified with these sacrifices,

> but the heavenly things themselves with better sacrifices than these. For Christ did not enter a sanctuary made with human hands that was only a copy of the true one; he entered heaven itself, now to appear for us in God's presence." (Hebrews 9:23–24)

Based on the Hebrews author's inspired statements, the temple in heaven was the original. Unlike the tabernacle and temples on the earth, it was built by the Lord Himself, not by man.

It is the prototype for the one on earth. The buildings that Moses, and later Solomon, and even later Zerubbabel and Herod, led in the construction of, were to be built exactly like the one God had already built in heaven. My assumption here is that this is because what would be built on earth would foreshadow God's glorious work on earth through His Son Jesus, and later the powerful and precious ministry of the Holy Spirit.

It is not my purpose to provide great detail about the highly skilled construction nor the great typology of these dwellings in this book, but those who have studied and preached and taught and written about the tabernacle and the temple have given us many wonderful studies of how the glories of Christ can be seen in these buildings. *I want to stay focused on the goal of this writing, which is to chronicle and document the revelation God has given in His Word that He has always, and will always, make provision to* ***dwell with mankind*** *in one way or another.*

4

The Tabernacle

The Tabernacle that God instructed Moses to build was a special place, an extremely significant place. It is the first place in scripture, since the Garden of Eden, that God chose to "dwell." A whole lot of Bible history occurs between the events of Genesis 1-3 where God is seen to be in the garden with Adam and Eve, and the events described in the Book of Exodus, where God speaks to Moses about building Him a "sanctuary".

Just a Little Bit of History ...

As you read the early chapters of Genesis, you will witness the proliferation of humanity and evil on the earth. The evil heart and sinfulness of mankind leads to the destruction of the world through the Flood of Noah's days. Life begins anew with Noah's family, and Genesis 10-11 informs us of the increase of people on the earth and the development of nations across the earth. The story of Abraham is told in chapters 11-25. Beginning in chapter 21 the Bible gives us the saga of the birth of Abraham's promised son Isaac, followed by the history of the descendants of Abraham. That story ends in Egypt, with Abraham's descendants becoming a family of 70 persons, including his twelve sons, the story of Joseph, and the Israelites spending 430 years in bondage in the nation of Egypt. During that time, Israel increases to such a large nation of people, that they become a perceived threat to their host nation.

Enter Moses ... and the plot thickens. Moving forward at break-neck speed, and to make a long story short, we observe how God uses Moses as a deliverer for His people Israel. After ten horrendous plagues, including the Passover in Egypt, Moses and God's people, about two million of them, find themselves freed from Egyptian bondage, out in the Wilderness of Sinai on the way to The Promised land. This story is told in the first twenty-five chapters of Exodus.

In the twenty-fifth chapter, God tells Moses

"Then have them make a sanctuary for
me, and I will dwell among them.
Make this tabernacle and all its furnishings exactly
like the pattern I will show you." (Exodus 25:8-9)

Please note carefully God's choice of wording in this passage: (cited above)

*"make a **sanctuary** for me, and I will **dwell** among them."*
(italics and bold emphasis mine)

Interestingly, there is an earlier reference in the Exodus text, prior to God even giving this instruction, found in Exodus 15, where we find a song of deliverance just after they crossed the Red Sea.

> "You will bring them in and plant them on the mountain of your inheritance— the place, Lord, you made for your **dwelling**, the **sanctuary**, Lord, your hands established." (Exodus 15:17 - emphasis mine).

Again, note carefully the terminology found there: "the place, Lord, you made for your **dwelling**, the **sanctuary**," (emphasis mine). It is the same as the wording used later in Exodus 25. It is my perception that this was possibly a *prophetic word* on Moses' part, sung spontaneously and inspired by the Spirit of God, foreshadowing what God was about to do for His people.

Now ... to The Tabernacle ...

Ordered by the LORD himself, prescribed to be built precisely according to a divine pattern, it's construction was sovereignly designed and very carefully directed for the express purpose of becoming God's temporary home on earth, His "dwelling place", with His chosen people. When it was completed according to His plan, there would be supernatural, but physical, manifestations of His presence. This would be a tent-structure, but extremely elaborate and costly, and would be amazingly portable. God would see to it that intense attention be focused on the project.

The Commissioning of the Project – Exodus 25-31

Beginning at Exodus 25, God commissions the collection of materials for the construction of this special place. Here, in the next seven chapters, He details every type of material, the colors, the dimensions, along with their purpose and use, and emphasizes again and again that it must be built according to the pattern He gave Moses on the mountain. In chapter 31, God even designates who will oversee the construction and do all the skillful work required, stating that he had specifically chosen, appointed, and filled these men with His Spirit and qualified and equipped them to do the work.

Four chapters later, in Exodus chapters 35–39, covering five chapters in our English Bibles, (originally written in the Hebrew language without chapter divisions) God orders and journals the actual construction; here we have the detail-by-detail building of this sanctuary for God.

Near the end of Exodus, to conclude chapter 39, with only one chapter remaining, we are given a summary that details the finishing of the project:

"And so at last the Tabernacle was finished.
The Israelites had done everything just as
the Lord had commanded Moses.
And they brought the entire Tabernacle to Moses:
the sacred tent with all its furnishings,"
(Exodus 39:32–33 NLT)

In these concluding verses of that chapter (and of the entire book!) every piece of furniture and every single part of the Tabernacle is named, and followed by these words:

"So the people of Israel followed all of the
Lord's instructions to Moses.
Then Moses inspected all their work.
When he found it had been done just as
the Lord had commanded him,
he blessed them."
(Ex. 39:42–43 NLT)

Set-up Time for the Big Project

Upon completion of the construction of all the parts of the Tabernacle, Moses proceeded to set up the Tabernacle. Again, in the final chapter of Exodus, we are told that he did it according to God's explicit instructions.

"Moses proceeded to do everything
just as the Lord had commanded him.
So the Tabernacle was set up on the first day
of the first month of the second year."
"So at last Moses finished the work."
(Ex.40:16–17, and 33 NLT)

God shows up at the Tabernacle ...

To crown the obedience of Moses, and in recognition of his absolute diligence to every detail God had commanded, God came to earth again.

To be with man.
To dwell.
To "tabernacle" with His people.

We read in verses 34-35,

> Then the cloud covered the Tabernacle,
> and the glory of the Lord filled the Tabernacle.
> Moses could no longer enter the Tabernacle
> because the cloud had settled down over it,
> and the glory of the Lord filled the Tabernacle.
> (Exodus 40:34-35 NLT)

When He was giving instructions (back in Exodus 25) for the construction of the ark, which would be the most important piece of holy furniture that would occupy the most holy place, God had promised ...

> "I will meet with you there
> and talk to you from above the atonement cover
> between the gold cherubim that hover
> over the Ark of the Covenant.
> From there I will give you my commands
> for the people of Israel."
> (Exodus 25:22 NLT)

It's A Lot to Think About, I Know ...

An observation at this point. It seems like the details will never end, becoming tedious to follow; and, unless one is a passionate, committed, Bible student who always presses on and reads the details no matter what, they might just check out at this point and say, "What's the point, anyway?" I believe that many people choose to skip lots of details in the scriptures, in their Bible reading, and often do indeed "miss the point!" Bear with me a little while longer here, and it will all come together, I promise. And later in the book, when *all* the pieces come together, there is a wonderful truth to be discovered, along with seeing the great lengths God has gone to make it all possible.

Recently while browsing in Facebook, I came across a friend's commentary that referenced the tabernacle in the book of Numbers. I posted the following comment on Facebook in response:

Charles F. Smith The Tabernacle is one of the major pieces of a great jigsaw puzzle that has composite pieces scattered from Exodus to Revelation. When all the pieces are found, put in their proper place, and seen together, a beautiful picture emerges, showing us that God has chosen down through the centuries, and even into the future, that it is His full intention to dwell with us on the earth.

Continuing-on into Numbers and Hebrews ...

Finally, the display of information about the tabernacle continues on into the book of Numbers. The tabernacle is referred to hundreds of years later in the New Testament book, Hebrews. Numbers chapter 7 begins like this:

"On the day Moses set up the Tabernacle,
he anointed it and set it apart as holy,
the Holy Place of the Lord.
He also anointed and set apart all its furnishings
and the altar with its utensils.
Then the leaders of Israel—the tribal leaders
who had registered the troops—
came and brought their offerings. Together they
brought six large wagons and twelve oxen.
There was a wagon for every two leaders
and an ox for each leader.
They presented these to the Lord in front of the Tabernacle."
(Numbers 7:1-3 NLT)

In the New Testament book, Hebrews, we find these reflections:
"Now the first covenant had regulations for worship
and also an earthly sanctuary. A tabernacle
was set up." (Hebrews 9:1–2)

"Now the main point of what we are saying is this:
We do have such a high priest,
who sat down at the right hand of the
throne of the Majesty in heaven,
and who serves in the sanctuary,
the true tabernacle set up by the Lord,
not by a mere human being." (Hebrews 8:1–2)

The writer further explains:

They serve at a sanctuary that is a copy
and shadow of what is in heaven.
This is why Moses was warned when he
was about to build the tabernacle:
"See to it that you make everything according to the
pattern shown you on the mountain." (Hebrews 8:5)

A Question to Ponder ...

Now – of all the information I have shared here, what is the most important thing about the Tabernacle?

For the purposes of this book, it is that God went to great lengths to ensure that there would be a place on earth, not just in heaven, where He could dwell with man. It would be durable and portable, but of unique and exquisite design. And, it would be patterned after what already existed in Heaven! He wanted man to know that He had *chosen* to dwell among His people, and that there would be a specific location on earth where He would choose to place His glory. And it gets so much more fascinating as we move through all the biblical revelation of how He has done this over the centuries, right up until the present time, and will continue to do so on into eternity!

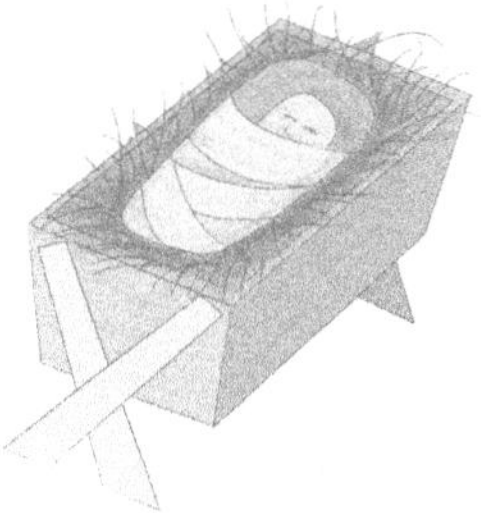

5

Jesus Was God's Temple

There is a story about Jesus told by the Gospel writer John, that establishes the truth of what I am sharing with you in this chapter. It is found in John 2:13–22.

In the Gospel of John, early in his account of the life of Jesus, in the second chapter, John recounts the day Jesus went into the temple court at the preparation of Passover and drove out the moneychangers. Impassioned by His zeal for God, He called it His "Father's House". It is in this event that Jesus makes a prophetic declaration in which He identifies Himself as the temple of God. The actual physical temple that stood in Jesus' day (1st Century A.D.) was Herod's Temple. It dated back several hundred years to the time when Cyrus the Persian allowed the Jews to return from Babylon following the Exile, to rebuild their temple. The governor Zerubbabel had led in the building of this temple. See Ezra 3:8. Some four hundred-plus years later, King

Herod had begun to refurbish this temple and the work had been in progress for forty-six years.

Here is the scene recorded in John's Gospel in the NLT translation:

Jesus Clears the Temple

It was nearly time for the Jewish Passover celebration, so Jesus went to Jerusalem. In the Temple area he saw merchants selling cattle, sheep, and doves for sacrifices; he also saw dealers at tables exchanging foreign money. Jesus made a whip from some ropes and chased them all out of the Temple. He drove out the sheep and cattle, scattered the money changers' coins over the floor, and turned over their tables. Then, going over to the people who sold doves, he told them, "Get these things out of here. Stop turning my Father's house into a marketplace!"

Then his disciples remembered this prophecy from the scriptures: "Passion for God's house will consume me."

But the Jewish leaders demanded, "What are you doing? If God gave you authority to do this, show us a miraculous sign to prove it."

> "All right," Jesus replied. "Destroy this temple, and in three days I will raise it up."
>
> "What!" they exclaimed. "It has taken forty-six years to build this Temple, and you can rebuild it in three days?" ***But when Jesus said "this temple," he meant his own body.*** After he was raised from the dead, his disciples remembered he had said this, and they believed both the scriptures and what Jesus had said. (John 2:13–22 NLT emphasis added)

So, in reflecting on Jesus' words to the Jewish authorities, what did He actually say? He said, "Destroy this temple, and in three days I will raise it up," (2:19). And in this response, the authorities understood Him to say that if they were to destroy this glorious building complex called Herod's Temple, the very center of their religious life and faith, that He was able to "rebuild" it back in a period of three days. As they react in their misunderstanding, they erroneously perceive that He is saying that what took forty-six years to do, He says He can do in three days! It is easy to understand their cynical skepticism and disbelief. But what Jesus was saying was something very different. He wasn't referring to Herod's Temple, the architectural accomplishment that took forty-six years to build, and that was, even then, still under construction. He was referring to His own body, and the resurrection that He was going to accomplish three days after His death.

His answer was in response to a question they had challenged Him with because of His actions in the temple:

> "But the Jewish leaders demanded, "What are you doing? If God gave you authority to do this, show us a miraculous sign to prove it." (John 2:18 NLT)

Therefore, He gave them a sign, the sign of His death and resurrection; but they had no comprehension of what He was talking about. And in His wisdom and understanding of God's timing for those events, He chose not to explain what He meant. He just made the statement and left it with them.

In verses 21–22 the writer / narrator John tells us,

> "But when Jesus said, "this temple," he meant his own body. After he was raised from the dead, his disciples remembered he had said this, and they believed both the scriptures and what Jesus had said." (John 2:21–22 NLT)

John's postscript to this story, cited above, is unequivocally clear. Jesus was calling His own physical body the very temple of God. Not only was this a revolutionary idea for the established religious culture, but it also had awesome implications for all Christ-followers then, and for all time, as we will see in the next chapter. We will examine the truth of the next phase of God's temple being in human beings through the presence and work of the Holy Spirit.

But let's not move on until we have looked more closely at the scriptural evidence for Jesus' claim that His body was the temple of God.

First, the Apostle John writes in the prologue to his gospel, the following words:

> In the beginning was the Word, and the Word was with God, and the Word was God. He was in the world, and the world was made by him, and the world knew him not. And the Word was made flesh, and dwelt among us, (and we beheld his glory, the glory as of the only begotten of the Father,) full of grace and truth. (John 1:1, 10, 14; KJV)

Second, later in his smaller letters near the end of the New Testament, John says this:

> **What Was Heard, Seen, and Touched**
>
> That which was from the beginning, which we have heard, which we have seen with our eyes, which we have looked upon, and our hands have handled, of the Word of life;
>
> (For the life was manifested, and we have seen it, and bear witness, and shew unto you that eternal life, which was with the Father, and was manifested unto us;)
>
> That which we have seen and heard declare we unto you, that ye also may have fellowship with

> us: and truly our fellowship is with the Father, and with his Son Jesus Christ. (1 John 1:1–3 KJV)

Now let's take just a minute to unpack this idea as it relates to my theme of *the dwelling place of God on earth.* John clearly states in his Gospel at 1:14 that God, in His preexistent state as The Word, became a human being and took on human flesh. This is the point of the prologue of his gospel, John 1:1–18, that He existed in eternity as co-creator, the source of all life, the light of mankind that would be manifested. It is clear from the two passages I've cited, that Jesus was the physical embodiment of the eternal life that existed with God and was indeed God from the beginning. He came to be and show us God's glory.

A third passage is found in the book of Hebrews in the New Testament. The writer of Hebrews says in Hebrews 1:3 that Christ is the "brightness of His glory and the express image of His person." (KJV)

Fourth, the Apostle Paul writes in **two places** in Philippians and Colossians, about Jesus' true identity as being the authentic revelation of God in human form: Colossians 1:13–15; and Philippians 2:5–11;

In the Colossian passage Paul states that God's son is "the image of the invisible God …" (Colossians 1:15).

In the Philippians 2 passage he tells us that God has highly exalted Christ because, even though He was equal to God in eternity, Christ humbled Himself to come as a human servant and submit to death in obedience to God's plan for man's salvation:

> "In your relationships with one another, have the same mindset as Christ Jesus:
>
> Who, being in very nature God, did not consider equality with God something to be used to his own advantage; rather, he made himself nothing by taking the very nature of a servant, being made in human likeness. And being found in appearance as a man, he humbled himself by becoming obedient to death—even death on a cross! Therefore God exalted him to the highest place and gave him the name that is above every name, that at the name of Jesus every knee should bow, in heaven and on earth and under the earth, and every tongue acknowledge that Jesus Christ is Lord, to the glory of God the Father." (Philippians 2:5–11)

Fifth, just one more reference from John's writings in his gospel, from Chapter 17, when he is citing the prayer of Jesus to His Heavenly Father just hours before his mob arrest, trial, and crucifixion; Jesus prays to the Father that He will be returned to "the glory I had with you before the world began." (John 17:5)

"After Jesus said this, he looked toward heaven and prayed:

> "Father, the hour has come. Glorify your Son, that your Son may glorify you. For you granted him authority over all people that he might give eternal life to all those you have given him. [3] Now this is eternal life: that they know you, the only

> true God, and Jesus Christ, whom you have sent. [4] I have brought you glory on earth by finishing the work you gave me to do. [5] And now, Father, glorify me in your presence with the glory I had with you before the world began." (John 17:1-5)

The reality is that Jesus was God in the flesh, on the earth, for a brief period of time.

As such He was the very "temple of God" on earth and literally housed the presence of God while here. One might say that "His presence 'tabernacled' with us in Jesus' human body."

This is an intensification over the way God's presence had inhabited the previous dwelling places — the tabernacle, the temple of Solomon, the rebuilt temple of Zerubbabel & Herod; this time God's presence dwelt in the human body of His son Jesus; and it prefigured the soon to come "indwelling" of the presence of God on the earth in the Body of Christ, made up of all believers following His death and resurrection, when He would send the Holy Spirit back to earth.

I will close this chapter with three more points that support the fact that God had come to dwell with man in human flesh, in the temple of His son Jesus. **First**, the prophet of old predicted that one would be born to a virgin and his name would be called "Immanuel", which means "God with us." (Isaiah 7:14) When Christ was born in Bethlehem about 700 years later, the gospel writer tells us,

All this took place to fulfill what the Lord had said through the prophet: "The virgin will conceive and give birth to a son, and they will call him Immanuel" (which means "God with us"). (Matthew 1:22–23)

Second, Paul writes in one of his letters to Timothy:

And without controversy great is the mystery of godliness: God was manifested in the flesh, … (1 Tim. 3:16 KJV)

And **third** and last, Paul's reference to Christ in Colossians 2:9, where he is warning the Colossian believers about the hollow and deceptive philosophy of human tradition, makes this amazing statement:

"For in Christ all the fullness of Deity lives in bodily form."

As we move on to the next chapter, we will see how God took the same Spirit that rested on Christ during His earthly life and sent Him (the Spirit of God) back to earth to dwell with us and to be "in us", making us the very temple of the living God on earth!

6

Now We Are the Temple

The twenty-first century finds us in a highly privileged place if we have put our faith in Christ and made Him our Savior and Lord. According to scripture, we are now "the dwelling place of God"! He lives in us! In His infinite wisdom and sovereignty God chose long ago to call a people to Himself who would become His Church, the Body of Christ on earth, to become a habitation, a tabernacle, a dwelling place on earth, through which He can continue to do His redeeming work throughout the world. There is a lot of scripture for this, but first I want to point you to Jesus; the thing He chose to focus on as the very last conversation he would have with His disciples on earth, prior to His death and resurrection, was His introduction to the Holy Spirit.

Jesus and the Holy Spirit ...

The Gospel writer John gives us the intimate account of Jesus' last few hours with His apostolic band of brothers in John 13–17.

In these chapters, Jesus heralds the coming of the Spirit, telling the disciples that it is to their advantage that He (Jesus) is about to go away, because that must happen before the Spirit can come. Jesus says,

---

"Nevertheless I tell you the truth. It is to your advantage that I go away; for if I do not go away, the Helper will not come to you; but if I depart, I will send Him to you." (John 16:17 NKJV)

Jesus took the opportunity on this most important night, according to John, beginning back at chapter 14, verse 16, to prepare them for the coming of the Spirit:

"And I will pray the Father, and He will give
you another Helper, that He may abide with
you forever—" (John 14:16 NKJV).

I encourage you to take time to read the entire account of those last few hours that Jesus spent with His disciples, chapters 13–17, and pay close attention to the many references to what the Holy Spirit would accomplish when He (Jesus) had sent Him (the Holy Spirit) back to earth. The word Jesus spoke is so revealing, given in the context of the coming of the Spirit:

"Jesus answered and said to him,

"If anyone loves Me, he will keep My word; and My
Father will love him, and We will come to him and
make Our home with him." (John 14:23 NKJV)

How was He and His Father going to do that?

By the Holy Spirit's indwelling that He was promising!

And then we should consider what was on Jesus' mind following the resurrection, in the forty days he remained on earth, until He ascended back to the Father. We get this story from the pen of one of Christ's closest disciples, John, and from St. Luke, the doctor who wrote the Gospel of Luke and the book of Acts. Let's observe Jesus in His resurrected, glorified state as He shows Himself alive to his fearful band of disciples. John reports in chapter 20 of his gospel, that Jesus commissioned them and breathed on them, saying,

---

"Peace to you! As the Father has sent Me, I also send you." And when He had said this, He breathed on them, and said to them, "Receive the Holy Spirit." (John 20:21–22 NKJV)

I believe that Jesus was preparing them for the next phase of God's plan.

Luke writes in the very first chapter of the book of Acts …

"and being assembled with them, He commanded them not to depart from Jerusalem, but to wait for the Promise of the Father, "which" He said, "you have heard from Me; for John truly baptized with water, but you shall be baptized with the Holy Spirit not many days from now." (Acts 1:4 NKJV)

Jesus went on to tell them that when the Holy Spirit had come upon them in a few days, they would receive spiritual authority and divine enablement (power) to become His witnesses, beginning in

Jerusalem, and then spreading the message outward from there (Acts 1:8). And then He ascended back to Heaven, to the Father, where He would shortly make good on his promises about the Holy Spirit (Acts 1:9–11).

Ten days later, as the disciples waited together in a Jerusalem upper room, praying and reminiscing over all their experiences with Jesus during His life and ministry, especially the most recent days following His death & resurrection, the Holy Spirit did in fact come in power and demonstration. The book of Acts records the coming of the Spirit at Pentecost, and then chronicles for us the continuing story of the Spirit's work, and the interaction of Jesus' disciples and those who came to faith as a result of their witness, with the Holy Spirit sent from Heaven. Truly, the "Promise of the Father" (Acts 1:4 NKJV) had been sent by Jesus, just as he had told them it would. In virtually every chapter of the book of Acts some identifiable act or work of the Spirit can be identified. I have often said, along with others I'm sure, that the book of Acts might well have also been titled, "The Acts of the Holy Spirit"!

The Holy Spirit in the World Today ...

Today, almost twenty centuries later, the Holy Spirit is still at work in Christ's church, also called "the Body of Christ" in the apostle Paul's writings (I Cor.12:27, Eph.4:12 NKJV). According to the New Testament scripture, God has chosen to place His Spirit in all believers individually, and the Body of Christ corporately, in order to have a residential dwelling place on earth during the church dispensation. A gathering of New Testament references makes this very clear:

"Do you not know that you are the temple of God and that the Spirit of God dwells in you? … the temple of God is holy, which temple you are."

(1 Corinthians 3:16–17 NKJV)

The Message paraphrase, by Eugene Peterson, puts it like this …

"You realize, don't you, that you are the temple of God, and God himself is present in you? … God's temple is sacred—and you, remember, are the temple." (1 Corinthians 3:16–17 MSG)

Paul also states the same truth with a further application in 1 Corinthians:

Or do you not know that your body is the temple of the Holy Spirit who is in you, whom you have from God, and you are not your own? (1 Corinthians 6:19 NKJV)

I love the way J.B. Phillips rendered this verse in his paraphrase as well:

"Have you forgotten that your body is the temple of the Holy Spirit, who lives in you, and that you are not the owner of your own body? You have been bought, and at what a price! Therefore, bring glory to God both in your body and your spirit, for they both belong to him." (PHILLIPS)

In his second letter to the Corinthians, Paul picks up this theme again in chapter 6. He writes:

"For we are the temple of the living God.

As God has said: "I will live with them
and walk among them,
and I will be their God,
and they will be my people."

(2 Corinthians 6:16)

The Apostle Paul also refers to the "indwelling" of the Holy Spirit in believers' lives in both Romans and 2 Timothy:

"But if the Spirit of Him who raised Jesus from the dead dwells in you, He who raised Christ from the dead will also give life to your mortal bodies through His Spirit who dwells in you." (Romans 8:11 NKJV)

"That good thing which was committed to you, keep by the Holy Spirit who dwells in us." (2 Timothy 1:14 NKJV)

Paul also teaches this concept in his explanation of the church being the Body of Christ on earth. Christ's Body on earth now, indwelt by the presence of God by the Holy Spirit, parallels to some extent the way that Jesus' physical body of flesh on earth (in the time and space of the first century), was indwelt and empowered by God's Spirit.

He says in Ephesians chapter 2:

"in whom the whole building, being fitted together, grows into a holy temple in the Lord, in whom you also are being built together for a dwelling place of God in the Spirit." (Ephesians 2:21–22 NKJV)

The Amplified Bible is very good in making this clear:

"...in whom the whole structure is joined together, and it continues [to increase] growing into a holy temple in the Lord [a sanctuary dedicated, set apart, and sacred to the presence of the Lord]. In Him [and in fellowship with one another] you also are being built together into a dwelling place of God in the Spirit." (Ephesians 2:21–22 AMP)

The apostle Peter also used this concept of the temple being built by God with the individual "living stones". The New Living Translation renders 1 Peter 2:5 this way:

And you are living stones that God is building into his spiritual temple. What's more, you are his holy priests. Through the mediation of Jesus Christ, you offer spiritual sacrifices that please God. (NLT)

In the closing part of the first half of Ephesians, Paul references the ministry of the Spirit as he prays a powerful prayer for the Ephesian believers. In chapter three he prays that they

"be strengthened with might through His Spirit in the inner man, that Christ may dwell in your hearts through faith;" (Ephesians 3:16–17)

If you think about it, isn't this the same thing Christ promised in Luke's final chapter?

"I am going to send you what my Father has promised; but stay in the city until you have been clothed with power from on high." (Luke 24:49)

As we come to the end of this chapter ...

In this book, we have been exploring the scriptures so far that show us how and where God has chosen to live and dwell in the earth and among His people in ancient times, and now in the present time. It is amazing that God has chosen to **always** "tabernacle" with us, whether it was the Garden of Eden, or in a portable tent called the tabernacle, or a glorious architectural edifice called the temple. And God even chose to dwell with us via "the mystery of godliness," as Paul described it in 1 Timothy 3:16, ("manifested in the flesh ...") through the first advent and incarnation of Christ Jesus. And we have just been seeing, in this chapter, the ***awesome*** reality that God has given us His Spirit to "indwell" us. (I use that word "awesome" intentionally and emphatically, not simply routinely as the grossly overused adjective of the day!) He has done this so that He can be "with us" in an ongoing relationship which is wonderful, yet somewhat beyond our full comprehension. I love that passage in Corinthians where Paul speaks of the amazing things God has done and has even yet prepared for those who love Him, especially the part that reads, "But God has revealed them to us through His Spirit"

But as it is written: "Eye has not seen, nor ear heard, Nor have entered into the heart of man the things which God has prepared for those who love Him." But God has revealed them to us through His Spirit. For the Spirit searches all things, yes, the deep things of God. (1 Corinthians 2:9–10 NKJV)

As we move toward the end of this journey, there are at least two more important pieces of this revelation to examine: the second advent of Christ, when He returns in power and glory to literally establish the kingdom of God on earth; and a brief glimpse at the grand finale described in Revelation chapters 21 and 22. I am challenged as I anticipate sharing with you about the Second Coming of Christ, and the New Heavens and New Earth. There is so much to discover.

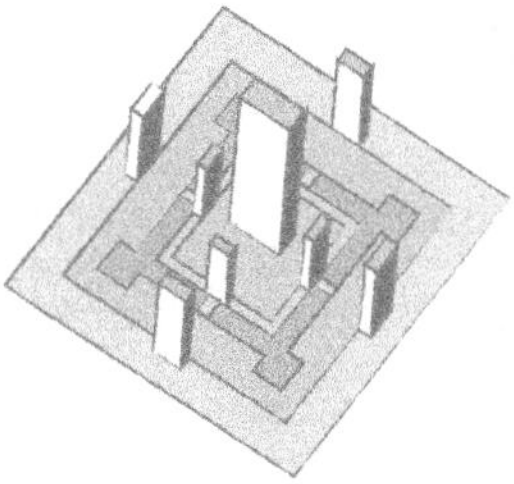

7

The Millennium – When Christ Returns

The Thousand Years

"And I saw an angel coming down out of heaven,
having the key to the Abyss and holding
in his hand a great chain.
He seized the dragon, that ancient serpent,
who is the devil, or Satan,
and bound him for a thousand years.
He threw him into the Abyss, and locked and sealed it over him,
to keep him from deceiving the nations anymore
until the thousand years were ended.
After that, he must be set free for a short time."
(Revelation 20:1–3)

Have you ever pondered the idea of life on earth without the devil present to cause havoc in people's lives? Can you even begin to imagine what it would be like to live on a planet where the prevailing culture, worldwide, is justice, righteousness, and truth? A place where Christ is King over all the earth, and God's agenda is the main agenda for all mankind? For ten centuries? A time on earth when death is more an exception than the rule, because people will be capable of living for hundreds of years again? In good health and prosperity? When the curse is lifted from the earth, and both the animal kingdom and plant kingdom are under the Lord's direct control? A time when despots, and tyrants no longer rule over men and governments, but Christ Himself will be King of Kings and Lord of Lords, and will have global dominion? Unbelievable? Given the conditions we face in our world today, yes! But, on the contrary – *no!* – not if you believe the Word of God! Because this is exactly what the prophets of old prophesied, and what is affirmed and substantiated by the Apostle John, as he shared what he saw in a vision on the Isle of Patmos, described in the final chapters of his vision in Revelation.

Jesus himself spoke of a time when things are going to be restored on earth, a putting-things-right again, as God wants them to be. According to the Apostle Paul in his writings in Romans, the creation itself has been

> "groaning as in the pains of childbirth right up to the present time" and "…itself will be liberated from its bondage to decay and brought into the glorious freedom of the children of God" (Romans 8:21–22).

When this restoration happens, God's presence will be

manifested on earth again, and He will dwell with us (mankind) again in bodily form, as was the case during Jesus' first advent. Christ's second advent, known by Bible students and theologians as The Second Coming, will follow a period of judgment when the vengeance of God is poured out on all evil on the earth (Revelation 6–19), and will usher in an era of peace and tranquility that is described by John the Apostle in Revelation 20:1–7. The expression, "thousand years" is used six times in these 7 verses. So, according to the Apostle John, there will be a "millennium"- a period of one thousand years, ten centuries, during which time Satan, the devil, man's and God's arch enemy of all time, will be subdued and put away, disabled from affecting life on Earth.

There is a time of restoration spoken of by Jesus in a conversation he had with the Apostle Peter and some other disciples, reported by Matthew. In this conversation, Peter is counting the cost of discipleship, and blurts out a question to the Lord, a question that all of us who have made any sacrifices for the Lord might have asked along the way:

> Peter answered him,
> "We have left everything to follow you! What
> then will there be for us?"
> (Matthew 19:27)

When Jesus answered his question, he made an amazing statement about the rewards coming to those who followed Him, but at the same time refers to a period in the future when things will be renewed and restored.

Jesus said to them,
"Truly I tell you, at the renewal of all things,
when the Son of Man sits on his glorious throne,
you who have followed me will also sit on twelve thrones,
judging the twelve tribes of Israel.
And everyone who has left houses or brothers or sisters
or father or mother or wife or children or fields for my sake
will receive a hundred times as much
and will inherit eternal life.
(Matthew 19:28–29)

I sincerely hope that you will take time to read this passage again, slowly and thoughtfully, and consider reading it in several other translations as well. Notice especially the reference Jesus makes to change that is coming when He says "…at the renewal of all things" in verse 28.

Consider the words of the apostle Peter in Acts in the New Testament. In Acts 3:21, he is preaching to a crowd of Jewish people who had been astonished by the healing of the lame man at the Gate Beautiful in Jerusalem and had gathered to hear Peter's words in Solomon's Colonnade (3:1–26); Peter has explained how prophecy had been fulfilled through the suffering and death of Jesus, the Messiah. As he calls for them to repent, he makes a statement about Jesus *remaining in heaven until…* (At this point in the story of Jesus, He has died, been raised from the dead, and after appearing many times during the forty days following the resurrection, has ascended back to His Father in heaven, and taken his position of power and authority at the Father's right hand.) It is in this context that Peter says,

"the Messiah, who has been appointed for you—even Jesus.
Heaven must receive him until the time
comes for God to restore everything,
as he promised long ago through his holy prophets."
(Acts 3:20–21)

Note the words of Peter in this Acts 3 passage ... (reformatting and emphasis mine)

"Heaven must receive him
... until
... the time comes
... for God to restore everything
... as He promised
... long ago through his holy prophets."

I believe that God has planned the time when this is going to happen. God already has it scheduled!

I love a verse I found in Isaiah's writings recently. The Holy Spirit showed me this verse and quickened it to my heart. It is found in Isaiah 60:22. The context is the redemption of Zion, the covenant people of God, the Jewish remnant which God will call to Himself and restore in the final days of history as we know it, when He completes the restoration.

"I am the Lord;
in its time I will do this swiftly." (Isaiah 60:22)

"At the right time, I, the Lord, will make it happen." (NLT)

"I, the Lord, will quicken it in its [appointed] time." (AMP)

Look at those translations one more time with me…
In its time … (NIV)
At the right time … (NLT)
In its appointed time … (AMP)

Heaven must receive Him until …

Heaven must receive him until the time
comes for God to restore everything,
as he promised long ago *through his holy prophets*. (emphasis mine.)
(Acts 3:21)

I hope you have taken notice of the repetitious references I have made to "the prophets" in this chapter. There is an amazing revelation in Amos' writings (another of God's Old Testament prophets!) Listen to what God inspired Amos to write:

"Surely the Sovereign Lord does nothing
without revealing his plan
to *his servants the prophets*." (emphasis mine.)
(Amos 3:7)

"his servants the prophets" ...

A variation of this, "my servants the prophets," where God claims ownership and oversight of the word of the prophets, is found repeatedly in the prophetic writings of the Old Testament, and then is affirmed and vindicated in the New Testament at the very end of all the revelations given to the Apostle John in the book of Revelation:

"But in the days when the seventh angel
is about to sound his trumpet,
the mystery of God will be accomplished,
just as he announced to his **servants** the **prophets**."
(Revelation 10:7 emphasis added)

"The nations were angry, and your wrath has come.
The time has come for judging the dead,
and for rewarding your **servants** the **prophets** and
your people who revere your name,
both great and small— and for destroying
those who destroy the earth."
(Revelation 11:18 emphasis added)

The angel said to me,
"These words are trustworthy and true.
The Lord, the God who inspires the **prophets**,
sent his angel to show his **servants** the
things that must soon take place."
(Revelation 22:6 – emphasis added)

I began this chapter with a series of questions.

They were designed to stimulate your imagination of what the world would be like when Christ is actually and completely Lord over all the earth, the time commonly referred to by some theologians and Bible scholars as *The Millennium*. These questions were inspired by what I have discovered in the messianic prophecies of scripture, the writings of the holy prophets, which the Apostle Paul referred to as "the foundation" of the church, which is the body of Christ on earth.

"Consequently, you are no longer foreigners and strangers,
but fellow citizens with God's people and
also members of his household,
built on ***the foundation of the apostles and prophets***,
with Christ Jesus himself as the chief cornerstone.
In him the whole building is joined together and rises
to become a holy temple in the Lord."
(Ephesians 2:19–21 – emphasis added)

In the remaining paragraphs of this chapter I want to pinpoint those prophetic scriptures that give us a sense of what life will be like when Christ returns and sets up His kingdom *on the earth*; at that time the prayer that Jesus taught us to pray will be completely answered and realized in the lives of people all over the earth:

"This, then, is how you should pray:
"'Our Father in heaven,
hallowed be your name,
your kingdom come,

your will be done,
on earth as it is in heaven."
(Matthew 6:9–10)

To restate Jesus' instruction, he taught us to pray that the Father's will would be done, that His kingdom would come … on earth as it is in heaven. One day that is going to happen. First let's consider some of the biblical references to the glorious return of Christ to the earth. Jesus himself spoke of this day, as he was sitting on the Mount of Olives (Matthew 24:3) and discussed His coming and the end of the age, in answer to his disciples' questions. He says in Matthew 24:14 that the gospel of the kingdom would be preached in the whole world as a testimony to all nations, and then the end would come. In verse 30 of that chapter, Jesus says:

"Then will appear the sign of the Son of Man in heaven.
And then all the peoples of the earth will
mourn when they see the Son of Man
coming on the clouds of heaven, with power and great glory."
(Matthew 24:30)

What Jesus predicted in Matthew 24 looks a lot like what Daniel the prophet saw hundreds of years earlier and recorded in his writings:

"In my vision at night I looked,
and there before me was one like a son of man,
coming with the clouds of heaven.

He approached the Ancient of Days
and was led into his presence.
He was given authority, glory and sovereign power;
all nations and peoples of every language worshiped him.
His dominion is an everlasting dominion
that will not pass away,
and his kingdom is one that will never be destroyed."
(Daniel 7:13–14)

Zechariah, one of the Old Testament prophets, prophesied of this day that is to come. I believe that most of his fourteen chapters concern the nation of Israel and their restoration as a theocratic nation under the Lordship of their messiah in future days. The fourteenth chapter is amazingly specific when he speaks of "a day of the Lord." I will not display the entire chapter here, but verses 3–9 clearly describe Christ's return to earth, to the Mount of Olives, the very place Jesus was sitting when He himself spoke of His glorious return, and the very place from which He ascended, when He left earth to go back to heaven. (See Acts 1:9–11)

> "Then the Lord will go out and fight against those nations, as he fights on a day of battle. On that day his feet will stand on the Mount of Olives, east of Jerusalem, and the Mount of Olives will be split in two from east to west, forming a great valley, with half of the mountain moving north and half moving south. You will flee by my mountain valley, for it will extend to Azel. You

> will flee as you fled from the earthquake in the days of Uzziah king of Judah. Then the Lord my God will come, and all the holy ones with him. On that day there will be neither sunlight nor cold, frosty darkness. It will be a unique day—a day known only to the Lord—with no distinction between day and night. When evening comes, there will be light. On that day living water will flow out from Jerusalem, half of it east to the Dead Sea and half of it west to the Mediterranean Sea, in summer and in winter. The Lord will be king over the whole earth. On that day there will be one Lord, and his name the only name." (Zechariah 14:3–9)

To this, compare how John describes Christ's second coming in Revelation 19.

> "I saw heaven standing open and there before me was a white horse, whose rider is called Faithful and True. With justice he judges and wages war. His eyes are like blazing fire, and on his head are many crowns. He has a name written on him that no one knows but he himself. He is dressed in a robe dipped in blood, and his name is the Word of God. The armies of heaven were following him, riding on white horses and dressed in fine linen, white and clean. Coming out of his mouth is a sharp sword with which to strike

> down the nations. "He will rule them with an iron scepter." He treads the winepress of the fury of the wrath of God Almighty. On his robe and on his thigh he has this name written: king of kings and lord of lords." (Revelation 19:11–16)

If one connects the verses I cited from Revelation, and the ones immediately following, verses 17–21, with the statement found in Zechariah 14:3, "Then the Lord will go out and fight against those nations, as he fights on a day of battle," it seems that these two passages speak of the same event. And according to verses 15–16 of Revelation 19, The "king of kings" will "strike down the nations," and "will rule them with an iron scepter;" To me, this indicates that Christ will seize control of the earth globally and will institute an enforced theocratic government.

Do you remember that little passage we are so accustomed to quoting from the prophet Isaiah every Christmas?

> "For to us a child is born, to us a son is given,
> and the government will be on his shoulders.
> And he will be called Wonderful Counselor, Mighty God,
> Everlasting Father, Prince of Peace."
> (Isaiah 9:6)

Consider the words that immediately follow in that same passage, in verse 7.

"Of the greatness of his government and
peace there will be no end.
He will reign on David's throne and over his kingdom,
establishing and upholding it with justice and righteousness
from that time on and forever.
The zeal of the Lord Almighty
will accomplish this."
(Isaiah 9:7)

The Righteous Branch Prophecy

There is also a messianic prophecy generally referred to as the "righteous Branch" prophecy (Jeremiah 23:5). Old Testament prophets speak of one whom God would raise up to rule in Israel in the future. (A future, which I might add for clarification, still has not arrived, and continues to await fulfilment.) The prophet Jeremiah refers to Him twice, in chapter 23, then in chapter 33.

"The days are coming," declares the Lord,
"when I will raise up for David a righteous Branch,
a King who will reign wisely
and do what is just and right in the land."
(Jeremiah 23:5)

"'In those days and at that time
I will make a righteous Branch sprout from David's line;
he will do what is just and right in the land."
(Jeremiah 33:15)

Isaiah speaks of this "righteous Branch" in chapters 4 and 11. And in Chapter 11, the references to Christ in this way are in the context of that most famous passage in Isaiah that clearly describes a different world than the one we know today:

"The wolf will live with the lamb,
the leopard will lie down with the goat,
the calf and the lion and the yearling together;
and a little child will lead them.
The cow will feed with the bear,
their young will lie down together,
and the lion will eat straw like the ox.
The infant will play near the cobra's den,
and the young child will put its hand into the viper's nest.
They will neither harm nor destroy
on all my holy mountain,
for the earth will be filled with the knowledge of the Lord
as the waters cover the sea."
(Isaiah 11:6–9)

The references to Christ as the Branch (in Isaiah's writings) are found in 4:2 and 11:1.

The Branch of the Lord
"In that day the Branch of the Lord will
be beautiful and glorious,
and the fruit of the land will be the pride
and glory of the survivors in Israel."
(Isaiah 4:2)

The Branch From Jesse
"A shoot will come up from the stump of Jesse;
from his roots a Branch will bear fruit."
(Isaiah 11:1)

At this point, I want to encourage you to read Isaiah 4:2–5, and all of Isaiah 11, together. This will give you a sense of the larger picture of Christ as the "righteous Branch", destined to rule righteously on the earth in the future.

… and just before we leave this idea to move on, let's take a look at just three more references …

"In love a throne will be established;
in faithfulness a man will sit on it—
one from the house of David—
one who in judging seeks justice
and speeds the cause of righteousness."
(Isaiah 16:5)

"You said,
"I have made a covenant with my chosen one,
I have sworn to David my servant,
'I will establish your line forever
and make your throne firm through all generations.'"
(Psalm 89:3–4)

And remember the verse from Zechariah that I have previously cited:

"The Lord will be king over the whole earth.
On that day there will be one Lord, and
his name the only name."
(Zech. 14:9)

Now let's consider the writings of the prophets predicting a world of justice, righteousness, and truth:

Remember that in Jeremiah 23:5, we found that one day there would come a King who will "reign wisely and do what is just and right in the land." In Isaiah 16:5, He would be "one who in judging seeks justice and speeds the cause of righteousness." Isaiah also tells us

"He will reign on David's throne and over his kingdom,
establishing and upholding it with justice and righteousness
from that time on and forever."
(Isaiah 9:7)

There is a beautiful description of the character and disposition of this ruler found in Isaiah 11, immediately following the reference to the Christ as the Branch from the stump and roots of Jesse. In verses 2–5 we are told that God's Spirit will be on him and that His rule will be based on *justice and righteousness.*

"The Spirit of the Lord will rest on him—
the Spirit of wisdom and of understanding,

the Spirit of counsel and of might,
the Spirit of the knowledge and fear of the Lord—
and he will delight in the fear of the Lord.
He will not judge by what he sees with his eyes,
or decide by what he hears with his ears;
but with righteousness he will judge the needy,
with justice he will give decisions for the poor of the earth.
He will strike the earth with the rod of his mouth;
with the breath of his lips he will slay the wicked.
Righteousness will be his belt
and faithfulness the sash around his waist."
(Isaiah 11:2–5)

I think this passage (particularly verses 2–3) has been often applied to Jesus in his first advent and time of ministry on earth in the first century; and rightly so, but I'm also quite certain that verse 4 has ***not*** been fulfilled ("He will strike the earth with the rod of his mouth; with the breath of his lips he will slay the wicked.") And it ***does*** fit the character of Christ as the coming king who will set things right and restore all things to God's original intentions. And when examined in the context of the entire passage from Isaiah chapter 10, verse 20, through chapter 12, verse 6, i.e. (10:20 – 12:6) it makes for a fitting description for the one who will reign during the Millennium.

Following is a brief analysis of the passage I just cited: Isaiah 10:20 – 12:6;

1. In 10:20 Isaiah prophesies of a coming day when the remnant of Israel, qualifying who this is as "the survivors

of the House of Jacob", will "truly rely on the LORD, the Holy One of Israel";

2. Geographically, he also identifies this group of people in 10:24, as "my people who live in Zion (which was another name for all the area in and around Jerusalem, including Mount Zion and the region of Judea); and in 10:32 Isaiah references "the mount of the Daughter of Zion, at the hill of Jerusalem."
3. In 10:22–23 Isaiah describes the destruction that God has decreed in the land, and in verses 25–34 he prophesies total victory.

   (Allow me to make an observation here. It would seem through simple logic that Isaiah's prophecies were time-stamped for *only* that historical period: i.e. that God will get total victory over "the Assyrians". For clarification, see Isaiah 10:5, 10:12, and 10:24. Consequently, it *seems* that **all** of this is in the context of the 6th and 7th century BC history of the Jewish nation. This would include the fall of Jerusalem, the destruction of the first temple, and the Exile of the nation of Judah by the Babylonians. This all sounds feasible, until we look into Isaiah's prophecies of a "Branch" in 11:1–16, which require us to look far into future, even beyond our present day!)
4. In 11:1–5 Isaiah prophesies of one to come in the future who would judge and rule and make decisions with justice and righteousness; One who would be anointed

with God's Spirit to have wisdom and understanding, the ability to counsel and the authority to act, One who would delight in honoring God and would absolutely know what to do in every situation.

5. And in verses 4 and 5, this "Branch", this "shoot that will come from the stump of Jesse;" this "Root of Jesse" (Isaiah 11:10) will "strike the earth with the rod of his mouth;" and "with the breath of his lips he will slay the wicked" (Isaiah 11:4); *I can assure you that this has not yet been fulfilled!*
6. Continuing our examination of 10:20 – 12:6, at verse 10 of chapter 11, Isaiah describes how that the Root of Jesse (which is Christ) will stand as a banner (a rallying point?) for His people (and I believe that means Jew and Gentile alike, all who have called on the name of the Lord to be saved); and the place of his rest will be glorious. In verse 11, Isaiah states that "in that day" (a time period yet to unfold completely) the Lord will "reach out his hand a second time to reclaim his people".
7. This is an amazing passage! As Isaiah continues we learn several things about that future day:

   First, again in verse 12 (see 11:12) Isaiah *repeats* and *says a second time* that this heir to the throne of David, "the Root of Jesse", "the Branch", will raise a banner … this time, "for the nations", and will "gather the exiles of Israel". For emphasis Isaiah clarifies in the second part of verse 12, that "he will assemble the scattered people of Judah (the Jews) "from the four quarters of the earth," meaning literally from all over the world!

Second, Isaiah says that he will dry up the gulf of the Egyptian sea in verse 15;

Third, the Euphrates River will be broken into seven streams by a scorching wind from the hand of this God-appointed ruler to create a "highway for the remnant of his people that is left from Assyria, in similar fashion to the way God did for Israel when they came out of Egypt during the Exodus period.

8. Finally, in Chapter 12, (12:6) we find these words:

In that day you will say:
"Shout aloud and sing for joy, people of Zion,
for great is the Holy One of Israel among you."
(Isaiah 12:1, 4, and 6)

The six verses in Isaiah 12 are broken down into two couplets of three verses each, and comprise a song of praise which Isaiah prophesies they will sing; and both couplets are preceded and introduced by the words "*In that day …*", (12:1 and 12:4) referring back to the description of the coming king who will rule the world with justice and righteousness.

In 12:6, Isaiah says that "the Holy One of Israel" is "among you". I believe that according to this passage, (and the many others I have previously cited):

> that *God will once again dwell on the earth in His resurrected and glorified Son, Jesus Christ,* in the glory of His Second Advent and thousand-year reign, just as Revelation 20:1–10 describes!

Consider the passage that immediately *precedes* chapter 12.

Look at **11: 6–9**, which is **the classic passage** that describes what I believe to be the Millennial period.

"The wolf will live with the lamb,
the leopard will lie down with the goat,
the calf and the lion and the yearling together;
and a little child will lead them.
The cow will feed with the bear,
their young will lie down together,
and the lion will eat straw like the ox.
The infant will play near the cobra's den,
and the young child will put its hand
into the viper's nest.
They will neither harm nor destroy
on all my holy mountain,
for the earth will be filled with
the knowledge of the Lord
as the waters cover the sea."
(Isaiah 11:6–9)

Finally, regarding a temple during this one-thousand-year reign during Christ's Second Advent, two major prophetic themes and concepts are key to our understanding. One is the concept of "the mountain of the Lord" in the "last days", and the other is Ezekiel's description of a temple found in Ezekiel chapters 40–48.

There are multiple references to "the mountain of the Lord" which speaks of the place where God will focus His energies and attention in the final days. Isaiah, Micah, Zechariah, and Ezekiel all refer to this in connection with end-time or last-days prophecies.

Here **Isaiah** speaks of this mountain:

> The Mountain of the LORD
>
> This is what Isaiah son of Amoz saw concerning Judah and Jerusalem:
>
> In the last days
>
> the mountain of the LORD's temple will be established
> as the highest of the mountains;
> it will be exalted above the hills,
> and all nations will stream to it.
>
> Many peoples will come and say,
>
> "Come, let us go up to the mountain of the LORD,
> to the temple of the God of Jacob.
> He will teach us his ways,

> so that we may walk in his paths."
> The law will go out from Zion,
> the word of the LORD from Jerusalem.
> He will judge between the nations
> and will settle disputes for many peoples.
> They will beat their swords into plowshares
> and their spears into pruning hooks.
> Nation will not take up sword against nation,
> nor will they train for war anymore.
>
> (Isaiah 2:1-4)

(And the prophet **Micah** confirms this word *identically* from Isaiah in Micah 4:1–3.)

Then consider what the prophet **Zechariah** says:

> This is what the LORD says: "I will return to Zion and dwell in Jerusalem. Then Jerusalem will be called the Faithful City, and the mountain of the LORD Almighty will be called the Holy Mountain." (Zechariah 8:3)

And what the prophet **Ezekiel** prophesies is confirmation as well:

> "'As for you, people of Israel, this is what the Sovereign LORD says: Go and serve your idols, every one of you! ***But afterward*** you will surely listen to me and no longer profane my holy

> name with your gifts and idols. *For on my holy mountain, the high mountain of Israel, declares the Sovereign LORD, there in the land* all the people of Israel will serve me, and there I will accept them. ***There*** I will require your offerings and your choice gifts, along with all your holy sacrifices. I will accept you as fragrant incense ***when I bring*** *you out from the nations and gather you from the countries where you have been scattered*, and ***I will be proved holy through you*** in the sight of the nations."
>
> (Ezekiel 20:39–41 – emphasis mine)

As I referred to previously, Ezekiel also prophesies of a glorious temple that will be built. It is described in detail by an angel in Ezekiel chapters 40–47. The Second Temple (which, over time came to be known as Herod's Temple), built following the Babylonian Exile and Israel's return to Jerusalem, definitely did not measure up to the glory of Ezekiel's Temple, and fell far short of being the fulfilment of all the related events in connection with that temple. A very important statement comes at the very end of Ezekiel's writings, after he has described the city borders and gates where this temple will be. In 48:35b, in the second part of verse 35, Ezekiel declares:

"And the name of the city from that time on will be: THE LORD IS THERE."

And with this Zechariah the prophet concurs, when he

describes how the LORD will return to the Mount of Olives, and will be king over the whole earth, and the survivors of all nations will go up annually to worship Him in Jerusalem. To state the obvious,

the reason the city will have the name
"THE LORD IS THERE",

is because He (Jesus) will be there!

Conclusion

As I bring this chapter to a close, I must tell you that this has been a challenging chapter to write. To try to cover as many key passages as possible to make the case for a literal one-thousand-year period on earth with Jesus himself as the head of government, while at the same time trying to keep my thoughts concise and in conformity with the rest of the chapters in the book, has been a formidable task. As I finally am coming to the end of this chapter, and anticipating one final chapter, the rain is falling steadily just outside my window, and I hear the Holy Spirit whisper the words of Isaiah in my spiritual ear:

"As the heavens are higher than the earth,
so are my ways higher than your ways
and my thoughts than your thoughts.
As the rain and the snow
come down from heaven,
and do not return to it

without watering the earth
and making it bud and flourish,
so that it yields seed for the sower and bread for the eater,
so is my word that goes out from my mouth:
It will not return to me empty,
but will accomplish what I desire
and achieve the purpose for which I sent it."

(Isaiah 55:9–11)

And I am reminded once again why I believe the things I am writing about. The *application* of the passage just cited is found in verse 11:

"so is my word that goes out from my mouth:
It will not return to me empty,
but will accomplish what I desire
and achieve the purpose for which I sent it."

God ***always*** does what He says He will do! He always ***has*** … and He always ***will***!

8

The New Heavens and New Earth

As I come to this final chapter, and I approach the idea of God's final and eternal dwelling place, as the culmination and grand finale of His intention all along, I am so tempted to go in so many different directions. For example, I'm wondering how much I should talk about the traditional understanding of Heaven that is commonly shared by thousands, possibly millions of Christian believers. That leads me to wonder if we ought to look back at the host of books written in time past about what heaven will be like. Or should I delve into examining scripture on everything it says about the New Heavens and New Earth? In recent months, just since I began to write this book, there have been a number of new books about Heaven released by very popular authors; some of them address the idea of Heaven coming to earth, in the New Heavens and New Earth. The temptation for me is to also belabor and examine the ideas of the New Heavens and New Earth, and the event described in Revelation 21:2, when the Holy City, the New Jerusalem, comes down to earth from God.

But in order to stay focused, and remain true to my original task, I want to just bring you scripturally to the final stage of *God's dwelling places*, to the ultimate consummation of God's eternal plan, based on my understanding of the scriptures. Looking back, we have visited the places in the biblical record where God was said to have dwelt on the earth:

- the Garden of Eden,
- the tabernacle in the wilderness,
- the temple of Solomon,
- the Second Temple following the Exile and Return of Israel,
- the incarnate flesh of the body of Jesus Christ during His earthly sojourn,
- then the temple of the Holy Spirit (which is the church, the body of Christ on earth now).
- Last, we looked briefly at the temple yet to be built for the final reign of Christ on earth in Jerusalem described in Ezekiel 40–48.

This brings us to the very edge of eternity, and we must return to the book of Revelation's final chapters to get a sense of what God has promised. It is in Revelation chapters 21 and 22 that we discover God's plan for being with His highest creation (mankind), *eternally*. Thinking back to the beginning when God created the heavens and the earth – the universe – He chose to create man and woman in His own image (Gen.1:26–27) and gave them dominion over all the earth. And God was with them in a garden and fellowshipped with them. That is, He was with them until sin entered through the serpent's deception, and Adam and Eve were driven from the garden and out of God's presence, (Genesis 3). When we come to the very end of the Bible, to the final two chapters, we discover an Eden–like setting. There will be a "new" heaven and earth, with a Holy City that comes down from heaven to the earth (Rev. 21:2). The city is described in detail in verses 9–27. In chapter 22, verses 1–6, we are told that there will be a river (like there was in Eden!) that flows through the center of the city. This river will be bordered by the tree of life (again - as there was in the Garden of Eden!) that bears crops of fruit every month, and the leaves of the tree are for "the healing of the nations" (Revelation 22:2). By the way, this river sounds a lot like the river described by the prophet Ezekiel in chapter 47 (verses 1–12)!

As fabulous as the description of the new heaven and earth is, especially that of the Holy City, New Jerusalem, the greatest thing to discover is that *God plans to take up residence with His human creation — eternally*, forever, in a way that He never has before. Revelation 22:3 tells us that the throne of God and of the Lamb will be in the city; and in the previous chapter, John hears a voice from the throne that announces,

---

"And I heard a loud voice from the throne saying, "Look! God's dwelling place is now among the people, and he will dwell with them. They will be his people, and God himself will be with them and be their God. 'He will wipe every tear from their eyes. There will be no more death' or mourning or crying or pain, for the old order of things has passed away." (Revelation 21:3–4)

We are told that *God Himself* will be with His people. The dwelling of God will be *on the earth with His people*; literally, in person, on the new earth, forever. No more dying, no more crying, no more mourning, or pain; the old order will have passed away. This is an incredibly amazing truth that we all need to grasp! And believe! And look forward to! Just like the apostle Peter wrote about in one of his letters:

> "But in keeping with his promise we are looking forward to a new heaven and a new earth, where righteousness dwells." (2 Peter 3:13)

The Final Piece ...

Okay, here's *the final piece* of this great collage or mosaic that I have been sharing with you in this book.

Do you remember the many references to the existence of a temple in God's plan?

Do you remember how we have traced the concept of God having dwelt in various places down through time, whether it was a portable tent in the wilderness, or a glorious and magnificent architectural structure such as Solomon's Temple, or the incarnation of God in human flesh in Jesus Christ, or the Body of Christ as the temple of the Holy Spirit? Since Moses' time, God has always had a chosen temple, or dwelling place, a designated place on earth to manifest His presence. But it was always temporary in nature. At the end of all things temporary, when God makes all things new and we move from time into eternity, this is what we learn from scripture, reported by the apostle John in the final revelation:

"I did not see a temple in the city, because the Lord God Almighty and the Lamb are its temple."

(Rev.21:22)

There is no temple there! That is, in the ordinary sense of the word, as we have understood in the past! But scripture says that God and His Son Jesus Christ, the Lamb, will be the temple! As I see it, the symbolic and temporary dwelling places that God honored us with over several thousand years of human history will have reached their grand design and fulfilment. *God will be with His people forever, daily, and in person!*

The day is coming when all those who have believed the word of the good news of Christ, and have followed Him in this life, will have the pleasure of His company for eternity. I will close with these wonderful words from the One who gave the revelation of God's plan to dwell with us:

"Look, I am coming soon! My reward is with me, and I will give to each person according to what they have done. I am the Alpha and the Omega, the First and the Last, the Beginning and the End."

"Blessed are those who wash their robes, that they may have the right to the tree of life and may go through the gates into the city."

(Revelation 22:12–14, and 16)

Postscript

I love the way God works to show us new truths about Himself as we walk in fellowship with Him. I try to follow the leading of the Holy Spirit in my life on a daily, continuing basis. As I was writing this book, the Lord graciously led me to discover yet another reference to His dwelling places, that I had forgotten was in the scriptures. As I said at the outset of this book, in my preface … "I have loved God's Word (the Bible) for almost six decades now." And even though I have read and re-read through the scriptures many times, I am reminded of how easy it is to forget so much of what we have read! I was at least two - thirds of the way toward completing this book when I re-discovered verse 18 of Isaiah chapter 8.

> "Here am I, and the children the Lord has given me. We are signs and symbols in Israel from the Lord Almighty, **who dwells on Mount Zion**."
>
> (Isaiah 8:18 – emphasis mine)

I began researching the references to *Mount Zion* and all

related verses and developed an extended chapter that would have been included in this writing. But the more I researched, and wrote, and discovered and understood, about the importance of Mount Zion in God's thinking, the more I realized that perhaps it should be the subject of another book, or at least an extended essay or article that stands alone. I have come to see *Mount Zion* as having great prophetic significance for our day and the momentous days that lie ahead, as we live in the expectation of the glorious return and Second Advent of our Lord Jesus Christ.

I pray that this book has been a blessing to you.

C. F. Smith, Savannah Georgia May 2018

CPSIA information can be obtained
at www.ICGtesting.com
Printed in the USA
LVHW08*1000170718
584068LV00011B/337/P